SITUATIONSHIPS

Poetry
&
Prose

By:

SaeLah

Copyright © 2017 SaeLah

All rights reserved.

ISBN:1981284699
ISBN-13: 978-1981284696

DEDICATION

To every lady involved in the making of this book. To loves lost, and love found. To the reader: may it edify you and administer grace to you. To those who have an ear to hear, let them hear.
-SaeLah

CONTENTS

	Acknowledgments	i
1	Situationships (Foreword).	3
2	Vertically Challenged.	6
3	Animated.	9
4	Manly.	12
5	Love Song.	15
6	El Color de Amor.	17
7	Sanctuary.	19
8	My Dove.	21
9	Evaluation.	22
10	Differences.	24
11	Confused.	28
12	Advice.	30
13	A-Muse-In Her.	34
14	The Fall.	37
15	North Pole (I).	42
16	My Everything.	46
17	In Time (You'll See).	49
18	Play No Games.	52
19	god Is Second Best.	56

20	Regrettably Yours.	60
21	Conversations.	65
22	Designer Clothes (Afterword).	68

ACKNOWLEDGMENTS

Mother. Thank you for raising and molding the man that I am today. Dad. Thank you for being the perfect example of what a man is. Lisa. Thank you for your protection and love ever since I breathed my first breath.

Mel, Phil, James & Kristin, Artis, Tramone, Darrell, Brandon, Matt, El, Myldred, Sanica, Kristi, Megan, Angelle, Justin, Karl Cole, and all my aunts, uncles, and cousins (TOO many to name)…you guys' opinion and encouragement is LIFE to me. Thanks for believing I could do anything.

Patrick and Ellisha, Tenesha, Glennzetta, Mieka, Dionne, San and Jakobe, Teshia, Jay, Charlene, Cormma, Keva, Nicole, Latoya, DK…your support brought this into fruition.

In Loving Memory:
Mother Rachel Bailey, Lee Payne Sr., Lee Payne Jr., Larry Babineaux, Yvonne, De'nard, Greg, Melanie, Cousin Rosetta, Drs. Artis and Debora Cash

I.

Steadfastness of Mind

1
..Situationships.
"...more than friends, less than lovers..."

I sat there. Alone. Confused...dejected and heartbroken with tears as my only companion. It happened again. Again I'd found myself picking up the eggshell pieces of a heart too freely given...so broken beyond recognition, it's hard to believe it was ever a lively organ whose every beat, beat with the purpose of loving *You*; whose existence was intentional in the way it bled rivers that flowed into the ocean of *Your* soul. I thought I'd burned the bridges to this place of desolation, but they now serve as torches lighting the way back. The feelings all too familiar. The loneliness all too acquainted with. The despondency all too accustom to.

Maybe it was my fault. Maybe I hadn't yet learned the intricacies of the complexity that is *Your* heart. Or maybe, it simply was never meant to be. No matter. Whatever the reason, I'm here now...here in this perpetual prison where the good times *You* and I had are replayed constantly with never a hope of being lived again. Too much has changed. The dynamic is different. What was shall never again be.

We were a living, breathing '*Situationship*,' defined by two people being in a situation that looks, feels, sounds (and the two act like they are in) a relationship...WITHOUT the official title and, quite consequently, without the commitment. Often one party wants more but the other party does not (they only want the benefits), so the aforementioned party settles for what they can get from the person they truly want, even if they are only getting hurt. "We walk into the sword just to feel the touch of the hand driving it through our heart." My older brother Clayton tried to tell me that.

---

*Our situation feels like a relationship,
but it's not.
Your actions say you love me but,
your mouth won't.
And all this time I was inclined to
believe our paths intertwined for a
reason.
Believing the season set before us
was nothing more or less than our
destiny made manifest and you,
well you were the sum total of
everything The Creator thought of
when He thought of everything I
could possibly need in this existence
called "life."
And in an instant my life was never
the same, the day you exhaled your
very first "hello" in my direction.
And at that second I melted;
any reservations, suppressed them;
friends questioned but I would second
guess THEM.
But Christon told me,
"Even second guesses have answers,"
and you were mine.
Took it as a sign the way our paths
intertwined like vines around the
Tree of the Knowledge of Good
and Evil...just a matter of time*

SITUATIONSHIPS

before I'd bitten what's forbidden,
uncovering what was hidden...
there's no hiding my affection for you.
But the intentions of your heart were
concealed; contoured too much to
recognize the real you, and this was our
foundation.
Still, I'm hoping I can **make up** for both
of our short comings in an attempt to
enhance the beauty I believe is under
there somewhere, so...
don't tell me I'm not what you want...
and don't lie to yourself, and tell me I'm
not who you need...

-SaeLah

2
Vertically Challenged.
"...she was nothing short of amazing..."

My soul had already known *You*. Before time was, back in the back of eternity past, *You* and I played tag and frolicked the fields of blissfulness in the mind of *The Creator*. Separated and stripped of our natures, we made pilgrimage to the present and our minds' eyes stopped seeing one another. *You* had forgotten me. Apparently, making the quantum leap from a place where no time exists, putting on flesh and coming to this matrix of tocs and tics, makes you forget. But knowing this, *The Creator* split the cure for amnesia in two parts, magnetized them, then hid one part in *You* and the other in me and called the cure "destiny." So now, destiny draws us together in the most animated way of sorts.

When I saw *You* again for the first time, my soul played leap frog behind the confines of my flesh, probably obsessed over what it already knew but my mind had forgotten. There *You* were in bodily form, as beautifully lustrous as *You* were in *The Creator's* mind back in eternity-past. *Your* irises radiated a rare iridescence familiar of the fields of blissfulness. Consciousness unlocked, my mind's eye stared into *Yours* with no regard for public humiliation. I

SITUATIONSHIPS

just had to reintroduce myself to *You* for the first time..

Excuse me, miss? Hi :)
I know you don't know me and I'm
sure you get this a lot but,
how tall are you?
The only reason I ask is because
upon diagnosing your dimensions
I figure, you're nothing "short" of
amazing :)
and amazing's pretty tall...
but in fact, I think you tower over her.
Sort of like the way Freedom Tower
towers over every other skyscraper in
the New York City skyline.
And in the same way the World Trade
Centers were the centers for trade in the
western world, I hope to be the twin to
your tower standing next to you,
trading my love for yours until the
terrorists of love try their best to hijack
our happiness and fly it straight into the
love towers we've built.
But they don't know that flying a bomb
into our love will only fuel and ignite the
fire that's already there.
And ground zero, will be rebuilt upon
cloud nine.
And just like the trade centers of old,
the two shall become one, and that one
tower of love shall stretch higher than the
old and scrape the floorboards of heaven.
So again I ask, how tall are you?
Because to me, you can't be anything
"short" of amazing!
And amazing's pretty tall so it leads me
to think of all kinds of questions like,
How tall is your mother?
Does height run in your family?

Were you always so regal, so above
anything petty?
Are you finished growing?
And does it bother you when people
stare at your loveliness?
I apologize.
I tend to ramble when I'm intrigued.
Indeed, I've never seen your shade
of lovely.
Myriads of others have planted themselves
and have tried to grow to your heights
but have failed.
I hear it's hard to breathe at certain
altitudes.
But if you had to choose I bet that you
would opt for the highest heights
imaginable, because that's just in
your nature.
And I would love to date ya,
become infatuated and eventually
fall in love with you; and that love
will serve as the soil that will receive
my seed and we'll watch those trees
grow to heights higher than their mother—
nothing short of amazing...which
is saying a lot because,
amazing's pretty tall.
Others have tried to reach your height
and have failed...
I guess they're just
vertically
challenged.

(But anyway, I'm SaeLah...what's your name??)

-SaeLah

SITUATIONSHIPS

3
Animated.
"...we were drawn to each other..."

It was serendipity...a kismet connection created in the cosmos. It was destiny, not devoid of divine direction. It was the story of legend, told by the stars in heaven. Sages from ages old spoke of this magnetizing force called love. It was *You* the mystics prophesied about. The connection rekindled, *Your* soul remembered me once more and again we ran the hills of blissfulness. My half found it's other and was made whole.

Together again, we once more lived in a place where time was not. We existed in each other's exhale and lived for the other's inhalation. Our hearts were harmonious with the heartbeat of heaven. It *felt* "right" as far as feelings have courage enough to travel. We even finished each other's....

I saw my reflection in your eyes
which means that you were beholding
me behold the beauty that is you.
And we were eye to eye where each
other's eyes are the windows to an
open heaven, and a continuous kiss
is the only bridge between both utopias.

SaeLah

Let us build bridges together.
Invite me into your heaven and we
will roam as freely as Adam did,
clothed in nothing but perfection
and the glory of The Creator.
Let us not be ashamed of one another,
but let us aim to suffer the other's presence
in a way reminiscent of Christ;
and the whole of the host of heaven
is made jealous.
Breathless shall we remain, suffocating
the other's space, suspended in the
moment;
taking in the other's aura as through
osmosis until we two are not <u>made</u>
but <u>created</u> One.
His most prized possession;
the essence and seal of His workmanship;
His love perfected and made iconic;
ironic I'm haunted by a love so
uncommon and all I could utter are
the words "But I'm common."
And you?
Well, you're the polar opposite.
I often sit amazed at the fact we were
even drawn to each other.
I gaze looking back to a time I was
drawn to another, but The Great Animator
erased that desire; blotted out my imperfections
as though to hide them from you;
redrew the lines surrounding my heart
to make it big enough to house your affection;
He sketched my arms long enough to
engulf you with my embrace, as if my
arms were designed to be a safe haven,
safe guarding you from the let downs of
this life; and I was drawn to you differently
this time, then again, this time He used pen.
That means our being drawn to one another
is permanent.

SITUATIONSHIPS

*I am the Mickey to your Minnie;
the Aladdin to your Jasmine;
the Beast to all of your Beauty.
We are divinely drawn to each other
by the hands of The Great Animator.
Maybe that's why our love is so
animated.*

-SaeLah

4
Manly.
"...she speaks to the king in you..."

In the "honeymoon" phase of our newly blossomed romance, there was not a wrong invented that *You* were capable of committing, only rights; even *Your* wrongs were 'three lefts.' *Your* flaws were beauty marks designed to make *You* stand out. *Your* short comings, the tallest in their class. Even *Your* imperfections were perfect. But what was most gratifying, is the way *You* made me feel in *Your* presence.

Why do men cheat? In most cases, it's not because the other woman is "finer" or better looking. Generally, it's not because she cooks or cleans better. Much of the time, it has everything to do with how she makes him *feel* in her presence. Most times, she has found a way to speak to the king in him. She has found a way to make him feel his manliest.

*Since the beginning of time,
a man's deposition and genetic
makeup was to wake up to the one*

SITUATIONSHIPS

woman who seems to complete
him in every facet of life.
It has to be right,
they bask in the light and bathe
in the love given of the only One
greater than themselves—
together.
And whether or not the weather
permits, together they fit,
joined at the hip to never omit
or sever that niche
(the better the fit, the better the kiss);
and relevant hints on reverent lips,
speak of a knit, NEVER to split;
and every gift that's perfect's
from G-D, though seemingly odd,
they're peas in a pod--
Together
(three peas come together to form
one pod—
one pea for you,
one pea for me,
one pea for G-D).
So when holding you close,
emotions evoke a focusing hope,
reloading the yoke and the burden
of yearning and learning each other,
we journey together while turning
the weather from cloudy to clear
in the atmosphere,
no shedding of tears,
we're meant to be HERE—
right now,
in this place—
TOGETHER.
And together we lay...
And when you're safe and secure
In my arms—
That's when I feel the most
MANLY.

-SaeLah

*"And he pitied other men who
take for granted or will never
know THIS...
something real and genuine,
found only in the arms of
another...
selfless and selfish at the same
time..."*

5
Love Song.
"...your voice is like a symphony..."

In my very biased opinion,
I think your first breaths are the
greatest **song** ever written...
music, for all this mayhem and
melancholy;
iambic pentameter for all this
pain;
the most beautifully written **chorus**
for all life's casualties.
Hidden within your **half and whole
notes** are the **harmonies** of the
heavens, and quickly, you have
become the **song** of my life
written in the **key** of love;
the **soundtrack** to my soul
placed on never ending **repeat**.
You are my favorite **song**;
your eyes are my favorite **verse**

and your lips, my favorite **lyric**.
Let your touch be the **bridge** by
which I enter Eden.
My thoughts have been **revamped**
to believe in even the most
unfathomable fantasies—
unimaginable happenings because
every day, you happen to me.
Your **voice** is my favorite **instrument**:
beautiful and **acoustic** like the
12-string guitar I live to hold
so close to me...
caressing curves until we fit
so perfectly.
A jig saw fit, and you were the
missing piece to my masterpiece.
And now the Master's peace
and serenity dwell in our completion.
We make beautiful **music** together.
Music lovers love us and our love
is their favorite **song**.
The stars align and **dance** to the
rhythm of your heart
and **groove** to the **pulse**
of your passion, and I have found
life in your **tempo**...

-SaeLah

6
El Color de Amor.
"...tu eres la luz de mi corazon..."

*I am ever consumed with thoughts
of you in the bonfire of my mind.
And when the wind of your compassion
blows my way, it tips over and spreads
like wildfire until the essence of my
being is engulfed in yours...
nothing else matters.
Life is not life unless you breathe
into mine.
And with your every exhale I
exit hell and am ushered into your
Eden.
Population: three—
G-D, you, and me.
And we convene every evening in
the cool of the day, sitting at the feet
of The Father as He teaches us how
to love one another truthfully,*

passionately, violently; relentlessly.
So when I speak it limits me because
words tend to get in the way.
And as I stumble over them and freefall
in love with you over and over again I
realize, I love you with more than words.
With more than verbs, I love you in colors.
I passionately love you in red as you walk on
the roses of my love and with orange I
provide the warmth of the sun.
With yellow I guide your path with the light
of that same sun and expel the darkness.
I love you in shades of green because it is
my very nature to love you and to grow in
love with you.
With blue, I balance and calm you and take
your blues away.
There are streaks of indigo to let you know
my affinity is for infinity.
I drape you in hues of violet that robe you
like the royalty you are, for you are the
queen of my heart.
And all these colors harmonize and form
a white light to love you in, letting you
know my love is pure.
And at the end of this rainbow of emotion
I find only you, worth a price so far above
rubies the tag reads, *"Priceless."*
Our Father already paid it.
Before the foundation of time, He sent His
Son to claim it for us...
and the price was His life,
so now,
we live...

-SaeLah

7
Sanctuary.
"...in your heart, I find sanctuary..."

All of my thoughts have been completely
given over to you;
caught within your captivity, solely
surrendered to the sweet solace
of your sanctuary,
where I find sanctuary from the
dangers of love's let downs.
Your body then, becomes the temple
wherein I worship Our Creator
for having made you.
Please, as priest allow me to enter
that I may pay homage to the
King through his queen.
I will rejoice as I enter your
gates and try to worship
your walls down.
I want all of your glory revealed
that I may revel and be clothed

in its eternal weight.
Sweat,
from hours
and hours
and hours
of worship cascades and permeates
the temple.
I peer through the windows
of your soul, stained the most
beautiful golden brown
in ever an eye's history; and I
surmise mysteries of your soul
as I behold the whole of your being,
being one with the Father and His Son
and Their Spirit, so holy...
so boldly, I enter your inner courts
and pass through to the throne room
where The Creator sits;
and in you all's presence I was
made to sit; clothed in your essence,
tailor-made to fit; I praise the G-D
of heaven Who gave this gift—
You.
Your presence is a present for my
present—
neither past nor future matters,
only this now, suspended in time
as long as our Creator exists;
and He shall never cease or desist,
and neither shall this now...

-SaeLah

8
My Dove.
"...you are my dove..."

I have not seen sunsets more
beautiful, moons more brightly lit,
nor doves more lovely than that
which I have seen in you.
You are my dove...
the peace of my heart,
that winged creature of grace
and regality perched atop this
heart of bark,
hardened by the letdowns of
past loves.
But you have chosen to embark
upon the not so easy
and nest there...
and for that I am grateful.
Grateful unto the Father of all
fathers that He would entrust
His dove unto me...

-SaeLah

9. Evaluation.
(Haikus from the Heart)

Could this really be?
Did I fall in love again??
Hoping you're the one...

Are you an angel?
It seems you hail from heaven.
G-D must have sent you.

You are the most beautiful.
Unparalleled, no one can match it.
Drawn with the finger of G-D.

-SaeLah

II. Change of Heart

10
Differences.
"...lovers make the best friends; but friends don't make the best lovers..."

You blew into my existence like a hurricane, where the coldest winter of my life met *Your* fiery passion and it was there, that a whirlwind romance was birthed with no cognizance of conception—equally, no contraceptive for two unprotected, hurting hearts left alone in a "Netflix and chill" generation, each only wanting to heal, to be held, and to be made whole. Inevitably, somewhere on the road to redemption, hurting turns to healing and as we become each other's patient, the "Florence Nightingale" syndrome sinks in—I have fallen for my healer.

Determined to never again be hurt, I had resolved in my own mind to always be intentional and upfront as early as comfortable where matters of the heart are concerned. Gone were the days of being boyishly bashful, not effectively communicating my interest and consequently eternally damned to "friend zone purgatory." No...from now on she would know early on my intent. Ectopia cordis is a condition in which a newborn's heart is formed outside of their chest cavity. In most cases, the heart can be seen protruding through the skin. I know the sentiment all too well...my heart was on my sleeve.

   As time apart from the "the Ex" and time together with me increased, so did our affection for one another. Every possible waking moment was spent entertaining *Your* essence or breathing in *Your* aura. Three hour phone conversations consisted of seventy-five minutes of actual talking, the rest listening to *You* breathe because neither of us wanted to go and we'd already talked about everything there was to speak on in a day. "You hang up!" "No, YOU hang up!" was the game of our rekindled adolescence, only to end in, "stay on the phone until I fall asleep." This was it-- months and months and months of stolen eye glances, unconditional charity, text messages beginning with, "Hey You," and ending with winky-faces and "XO's;" friends trying to figure out if something was being hidden from them; *Your* mother calling me "son;" bonding with *Your* daughter; romantic Facebook statuses; jealousy over "likes" and "loves" that weren't clicked by *You*; forehead kisses, and countless other gestures prompted the wellspring of my emotions to spill over and "waterfall" from my tongue into *Your* ear. *You* HAD to know where I stood. So after an evening of alone time, chasing sunsets and watching the sun tiptoe away leaving orange and purple footprints in the sky for the moon to follow, I pulled into your driveway and attempted to arrange words in a syntax that would convey my feelings:

Me: So...listen. I know you are just getting out of that last situation with your ex a few months ago, and a couple weeks ago you admitted to me you are definitely TRYING to move on but you still get butterflies whenever your ex calls or texts. I can understand that, I get that. But are we good?

You: Why do you ask that?

Me: Well, ever since you admitted that to me, it just seems like something is off. Not a whole lot, but our interaction is definitely a bit different.

You: I know you're not completely confident that I'm over that situation, so how do *you* feel?

Me: I don't really think about him as much as I think about US and where WE're headed. So where does all that leave US?? Like, what have we been doing the past few months? Are we headed towards something, trying to build something together or are we just wondering aimlessly?

You: <Dramatic pause>

You: Wondering aimlessly, I guess…

Me: Wow. Ok…uhm, yeah. I kinda thought we were being intentional with each other, tryna build something. You'd always said you were done with him finally and wanted to move ahead with me, just give you a little time.

You: I just don't think it's fair to your to start something knowing I'm not completely done with that. And I HATE the fact I'm not done with it. But I don't know, when he calls or I hear from him, I can't deny I still get all these feelings. At times I'm like 'why did I ever leave him?' and then I'm like 'oh yeah, *that's* why I left.' It's like I'm not confident in any decision I make regarding him.

Me: <sigh> Yeah but you can't move on, until you actually *move on*. So what do you tell him, as to why you're not getting back together with him because I'm sure he's tried to? Do you tell him about me??

You: <Pauses, looking down>

You: I tell him he hasn't shown me he's serious. I need to know that he's changed…

My brain: ((Sooooo, if he shows her he is serious, she'll go right back to him, even though she says she knows he's no good for her???))

> *"Your words were like darts, daggers to the heart...and I didn't even have on a shield to protect.."*

11
Confused.
"...you can have all the boxes checked, and that person will still only look good on paper..."

Uhm, what just happened last night?? I woke up swearing it was the most godforsaken nightmare I could have ever endured. I reached for my phone and a text message solidified my already somber suspicion... *I am so sorry about last night. I never meant to hurt you. I really tried to love you. I still want you in my life. Can't we just continue how we've been doing it? It works for us, right?* It actually happened. My heart crumbled after months of learning to walk in love with her, only to find I was walking in the wrong direction...which explains why I am *here*. Here at this moment of melancholy, at this place of disappointment. Wrong direction leads to a wrong destination. But at what point did I get off course?? Therein lies my confusion...I know I had [almost] all the boxes checked...

✓ - List

- ✓ I want someone whose touch can chase away negativity
- ✓ I want someone whose voice can serenade my soul to a point of serenity
- I want someone who will not be afraid to let me love her fully
- ✓ I want someone I am not afraid to love fully
- ✓ I want somebody who makes me forget the past, get lost in the present, only to be found in our future
- I want someone who causes me to see the wind
- ✓ I want someone whose arms are regarded as a safe haven
- I want a partner...someone who realizes it's about the "team" and MAKING that work
- ✓ I want someone thoughtful and compassionate
- ✓ I want someone I can be proud to call the mother of my seed
- ✓ I want someone honest, who possesses integrity and won't cheat
- ✓ I want a supporter, who will only tear down (with words) for the purpose of building up stronger and better
- I want someone who looks at me every time after, like the first time she fell in love with me
- I want someone who believes I can do anything
- I want someone who comes into my life on accident but stays on purpose

12
..Advice.
"..there is wisdom found in the multitude of counsel"
(Proverbs 11:14)

Brent:
She doesn't care for you in the long term from a temporal perspective, let alone concerning what's honorable to G-D. That's not love bro. I don't have a long spill. There's a season of pleasure even in the wrong choice...but it never satisfies in the end though. Ask yourself what you believe about G-D right now...make the choice, even the one that requires patience in light of the truth of Who G-D is. It's not easy...I'm praying for you bro. I know the uncertainty and longing is painful but just know these afflictions are light and momentary. I hope you're not pulling an Esau from the bible, bro...don't pass on MJ for Sam Bowie.

Shamika:
You know what to do. No need for advice: cut ties COMPLETELY. Stop being a space filler because that's the

purpose you are serving. She doesn't have any regard for your feelings based on how she's handling it. She can't have her cake and eat it too. You need someone who wants you just as much as you want them and that's clearly not the case for y'all. She's clearly still hopeful of him and even if he never comes for her or if they try again and don't work out, I think she's not the one for you because she's always viewed you as a second best. Move on...Teddy P said it best: "I think I better LET IT GO! Let it go baby! Looks like another love TKO! Oh ho ho ho hooooo!"

Kaleatha:
Ok...here's the thing...I never expected her to put you in a situation like this! I'm trying to be careful with my words because it's easy to give advice when I really don't have room to give it because I'm in a similar situation. I don't wanna say just walk away but at the same time I think you know what you need to or should do, based off what you know. Your other friend said what she said because she's your friend and she doesn't know Her but unfortunately, she may speak the truth. I just wanted to see you guys together...didn't want her to miss out on an awesome man.

Samantha:
I honestly don't think you should continue to wait on Her. I am a woman and I know how we are in these situations There is a huge chance of you being hurt. I know you really like her, she's the best...but if she is openly admitting that she has feelings for an ex, I would let her sort that out. She won't be 100% committed to you all's relationship in her heart...that's not being fair to you or her. I know it's hard...it was hard for me to tell you that...BUT, I wouldn't have said it if I didn't know that I was right. Why would you even settle for someone who can't commit to you wholeheartedly? It's like you are saying "I'll accept whatever I can get," and that's not right. You are better than that. She can move on without him being COMPLETELY gone, but it's apparent that

she does not want to.

Jamarr:
Bro like I really think [She] is a good person but she's not where you at. I know exactly how you feel because I went through something similar a while ago. Deep inside you already had a feeling that maybe it wasn't gonna work but you probably ignored all the signs just like I did. You probably even prayed to G-D for a sign and ignored it also like I did. Bro you are way too good of a man (no homo lol) for her. You gonna have to make yourself less available because as long as you are so available, she has no need to commit because you're giving her everything now without a commitment. Honestly bro, you're gonna probably have to just back way off because you're not gonna be friends with her because you have deep feelings and may be in love. I promise you one day she is gonna regret this very moment just as the girl did when I went through this. Don't question yourself thinking what you did wrong. You was perfect for her. Just look at it as if G-D answering your prayers.

Evoni:

That's understandable though...even though it hurts, she was honest...at least I think.. You don't find that too often. Most people will pull you into a relationship knowing that they're not healed or moved on from the last relationship.. You don't deserve someone that's broken or still in love with someone else. I think sometimes we mistake missing a person as having to be with them. When it's actually just part of the process of moving on..

Mitchel:
I'm not even gonna tell you nothing wrong...MOVE ON BRO!!!! I didn't say don't be cool, don't date, don't care for her...just don't put any additional energy or emotion into her my nizzle. She is in a gray area in her head...she has the potential to really hurt you.

I've been there and done that...it NEVER works out for the new guy. Maaaaan...it's the way females operate. It's just too soon, homey. As long as a woman has feelings, the ex still has a chance...it don't matter how good you are to her. Hard to say bro...what I've learned in these situations is you have to step out of it and allow her room to choose...just don't be surprised if she chooses him. It's not her, it's just how love works sometimes...not always a happy ending.

Rena:
You need to leave her alone. She's already told you she's into the other guy still. Why do you continue to pursue when they tell you what it is or how they feel??

Justyce:
Wow! With that being said, you need to just back up off her and hopefully she will get it together before you or someone else sweeps you away. ("But it's hard!!") I know but you have to look out for your feelings too, though It will take time...sorry if you going through that with someone you really like.

Trish:
I'm going through a similar situation. And it's because they have somebody else who is their main priority. And we're like the go to person when so and so doesn't work out...sh!t...face it...we're the rebound!! And rebounds never win...honestly, we keep putting ourselves through heart break for no reason..

13
A-Muse-In Her.
"...it's all fun and games until someone's heart is broken..."

Clarity |*kler*-uh-tee|: (n) Free from obscurity, easily understandable; the comprehensibility of clear expression

It's been a couple months now. Each day is rehabilitation unto itself. "One foot in front of the other, one day behind another." Each day is a battle…some days won, some days lost. I have tried every possible quotient to our division: keeping you in my life, pretending you're my best friend merely so I can be around you (because a part of you is somehow better than none of you); I've tried not speaking with you because the pretending rips open the wound every time I'm around you (because all of you is definitely better than only having a part of you). I've tried to make sense of the past few months. I tried giving you the benefit of the doubt. I tried retracing my steps to see exactly when I walked out of your heart. I tried rationalizing your decision but always came up more confused by this new math where ME + YOU somehow does not = Happily Ever After; stuck in this 'love *triangle*' because you can't leave that *square* alone, but why can't you?? It's really starting to affect our *circle* of trust…but geometry was never my strongest subject. But then, a bit of clarity..

SITUATIONSHIPS

*I found inspiration in the eyes of one
who looks into the eyes of another;
and it took a while to discover what lies
in the cupboard or pantry of her heart
would burn in my oven.
See, I "Fahrenheited" the flames of my
love and she changed all a'sudden, and
changed into something so beautifully ugly,
but I couldn't see she had eyes for another
'cuz I was inspired by the eyes of my lover
(and nothing else mattered).
See, I thought I found a muse in her but
I was just amusin' her, and with every love
gesture I became her court jester, and she
remained my queen.
Wayne said, "It ain't trickin' if you got it,"
and she had it 'cuz I gave it to her,
though I didn't have it to give.
So who's the pimp and who's the trick?
Who ended up broke and needs a fix?
Me.
And the more I gave, she would receive
and the more enslaved to her I would be;
and the price that I paid never mattered
to me, 'cuz I was inspired by what I
would see, in the eyes of one who
looks into the eyes of another.
See, I found inspiration and a safe
haven in the arms of one who had
arms for another; she took a while
to discover that while I would hug her,
I knew she secretly simply wanted
to be held.
Most men don't understand the difference.
And every time I would mention
to her that I'm different,
she would smile with her eyes and
solidify my position—as "friend."
See, I thought I'd found my muse
in her, but I was just amusin' her,*

and with every love gesture, I
became her court jester and she
remained my queen.
I found inspiration in the presence
of one who longed for the presence
of another.
But by the time she discovers I'm
truly her lover, I'll be gone, having
found inspiration in the eyes of
another who only has eyes for me.
And I...well, I will have found my
muse in her, not simply amusin' her,
and with every love gesture,
I will be made her king and she
will forever remain my queen...

-SaeLah

SITUATIONSHIPS

14
The Fall.
"...falling in love is like falling...it's the same exhilaration..."

Question:
What's the greatest pain?
Some would say maybe a gunshot wound
to the body or broken bones,
but the greatest pain I've ever known
came at the end of a fifty thousand foot
freefall after jumping headfirst with her
off the pinnacle of love's peak.
And it was she who taught me to embrace
my fear of heights just before convincing
me to climb the backs of eagles with her,
and ride their wings to the very zenith
of our existence, our own
Mt. Olympus.
Living this close to the heavens,

*it was nothing for us to reach out and
touch constellations and write our
love in calligraphy,
leaving legacies and mysteries in the
heavens of a love perfected to dwellers
of a land uninhabited by love:
We Are Legend.
Numbered with the constellation greats
like Andromeda & Perseus or
Artemis & Orion,
yes! Our love, too, was written
in the stars!
And altitudes this high produce
palpitations that lie deep within
the heart but have nothing to do
with medical conditions but simply,
she's the reason my heart keeps
skipping.
Tachycardia dysrhythmia never
felt so good and at 1,000 heartbeats
per minute, I have never felt so alive!
She's opened my mind to infinite
possibilities, now I think I can fly!
So I swan dive with a half gainer
and full twist off love's peak
into love's abyss,
mistaking falling for flying;
but who cares about falling if you
truly believe you're falling in love—
it's the same exhilaration,
so it's easy to be mistaken
and as we plummet towards the
pavement, I look to my right and
make this statement:*

SITUATIONSHIPS

"Baby? I promise.
I'll love you if you let me.
And if I could be honest,
girl it's true, you have swept me!
Swept me off my feet, now tell me—
who'll love you better?!?
Fall in love with me, and you'll
be falling forever..."
And she simply smiled...
as if her smile was the substitute
for all the words she couldn't say,
words like:
"Let's just live in the moment;
because we don't know what the
next minute holds,
but we know Who holds it, so...
whatever happens, we'll be alright."
And at that I thought nothing of it,
because whatever came out of
her mouth I trusted and took it
as wisdom.
But if I would have listened
more intently at her statement
I would've discerned her words
were preparation and not words
of comfort but laceration
that would eventually lead to a
heart that is wounded.
She was right.
Because not even a minute later
I looked to my right and realized
now I'm falling in love
A L O N E...
and at a rate much faster than

9.8 meters per squared second.
I guess our constellation's no longer
a legend—
a map in the heavens guiding
dwellers of a land uninhabited by
love—No!
I guess this would make me a falling
star to be wished upon;
but I feel like a plant to be pissed upon
and my heart is forever marked as
your territory so, claim me yet again
because I never wanted to stop falling.
I truly believed we could have fallen
forever.
But maybe...maybe forever lasts
only as long as it takes to hit the bottom.
And the bottom hurts...this, a
deplorable fact.
And it hurts like...

like...

...

D**N...

I aint got a metaphor for that...
It just hurts.
But I do know, bullet wounds close
and broken bones reset and fuse
together...
but what of the heart that is
severed?
Severed in two and rejected?

SITUATIONSHIPS

*Rejected, and too, it's neglected,
and you?
Well you're simply left falling...
falling through the darkest,
blackest abyss called 'Love.'
And there's no worse pain than
being in love alone.
And the fall hurts.
It hurts, but it doesn't kill you.
It just leaves you wishing
it would have...*

-SaeLah

15
.North Pole (I).
"...how cold must winter be, for those with no warm memories and no one to hold..."

*Why is it that it's the dead of summer;
or maybe you killed us and now
summer's simply dead but,
either way it's feeling like
winter.
December.
And the present is no present
because your presence is as
cold as Christmas day.
Icicle silences break off and become
darts aimed at my heart,
sharp enough to kill any relationship.
The sun is out, but it's not warm enough
to thaw this frozen tundra romance
of ours.
Frostbitten, I no longer <u>feel</u> loved.*

SITUATIONSHIPS

*So in order to salvage my sanity
I need to amputate you from me;
cut you off like the painful hangnail
you are;
cut you off like when I'm talking
and you interrupt my thoughts and
expressions just to express you're
unimpressed with the direction
we're headed...
not even hearing I was trying to say
the same thing.
But the difference is,
you just present the problem;
I bring up the problem so we can
collaborate to solidify a solution
but the truth is,
I might be grasping at straws that
aren't even there...
and frankly,
neither are you.
So I set out on a search to find you
again because the same love that
should have brought you home
last night, is the same love that
leaves home to go and find you
this morning.
But my darling "Gretel" has left
no petals or breadcrumbs that
will lead me to her so could it be,
she doesn't even want to be found??
And I tried to be brave,
your knight in shining armor...
But you can't save the damsel
from her distress if she doesn't*

*want to be saved.
Believe me,
I've tried...*

-SaeLah

SITUATIONSHIPS

"So he fervently prayed to his G-D for a crash course in osteopathic medicine, hoping to heal her heart and nurse the wounds of the pain previously inflicted..."

SaeLah

16
My Everything.
"in the end, there will probably be nothing between us...and perhaps, that is everything..."

[John Keats]
*"A thing of beauty is a joy forever.
Its loveliness increases, it will
Never pass into nothingness..."*
●●

You are my forever;
my beautiful one,
ever remaining;
never waxing cold,
never fading away,
never varnishing;
my ever increasing joy.
You are all the wonders

of the world to me;
everything made perfect
is you.
You are the most
beautiful twilight
these eyes might ever
have held...
do you feel my eyes
caress you?
Can you feel my eyes
massage your soul
as I see into you?
I swim the pools
of your peaceful
pupils as if they
were the Pool of
Shalom,
and the waters were
stirred by the wings
of angels,
causing healing to
the hurt my heart's
felt by everyone
before you.
Love made anew—
there's no longer
anyone before you.
As far as I'm
concerned,
there's only been
you since the
beginning.
You, my forever who
has been,

*and my eternal
who will always be;
my beautiful one;
more beautiful than
1,000 summer
sunsets, set ablaze
to the horizon.
You are an eagle
in midflight—
majestic.
You are a leopard
midstride—
graceful.
You are a lion's
roar—
all power.
You are everything
to me...
the only thing you
are not,
is mine...*

-SaeLah

17
In Time (You'll See).
"...having eyes, they see not..."

Verse I

(The homeys ask)
Why I still chase you, why don't I just replace you?
Why I keep the faith when I'm knowing I can't change you?
Why I stay committed when you don't want me to date you?
They tell me I'm a square, try working from different angles, but...
That's the homeys, only looking out fo' me...
because they don't want to see my heart broken again.
They like, "You dope with the pen! Fam, get focused again."
But all I want to write about is how you're focused on him.
Won't lie, I cracked a smile when you broke up with him...
thinking what it meant for me now that it's over for him.
So now I'm celebrating like I made it to the end zone!
But on the real, I just made it to the friend zone ☹
If I was smart, I would have BEEN gone...

But cupid has me stupid, so "Ashanti" [I'm foolish...]
How'd I get here with someone I was just 'cool' with??
A heart's a house for love, I'm hoping that you would move in.
It's crazy, how much you trust me with your daughter
and that little girl's amazing, it's hard not to get caught up.
My dude told me "Chill! Before a ni99a get caught up!"
But if she's this amazing, who wouldn't want to be father!?
Thought I could be the one to bring you joy...
I mean, let's keep it real, who better for you than the boy??
You complain you know the struggle of being a single mother,
but pretend you don't know nothing of having someone
who loves you
(Right in front of you...)

Verse II
Reminiscing on that night at the park,
exchanged more than just a kiss, girl I gave you my heart.
More than just friends, you were playing the part.
I tried to be your light, you should give me your dark.
The next step, I don't have to mention:
I told you how I felt and you told me how you didn't.
I asked you what was next and why you're fighting the feeling,
and it's never been the same, you started to act different.
Yeah...I remember that night vividly.
I only pressed the issue to see where you were mentally.
Now all of a sudden you ain't sure if this is meant to be,
when just the week before you were claiming how much you're
into me!
It's cool...you're human and I guess feelings change.
I'm still learning, had to charge it to the game;
I'm still burning, guess I need a larger flame;
I still feel it though, that's a lot of pain.
Yeah...I tried to be your everything.
I wanted you to know that you're worthy of wedding rings.

SITUATIONSHIPS

I wanted you to know that your soul could be happy, your spirit could be glad, and your heart deserved to sing! So we remain "more than friends, less than lovers," Because you're too afraid to move on... I know you're thinking, "If it ain't him, who possibly could it be??" And I'm just over here waiting, praying in time you'll see (that it was me all along but...I love me enough not to hurt me anymore... (You ain't never gonna come around)

-SaeLah

18
Play No Games.
"...hurt people, hurt people..."

As one can imagine, the devastation sent me into a spiraling descent. Falling in love somehow turned into a suicidal freefall, knowing I would die upon impact at the place of rock bottom. I resolved in my mind that I would care nothing for anyone else's heart, as no one cared for mine. I would deny love for another as love had denied me. Remaining upfront, I let it be known from jump that I was "not looking for anything serious right now." I wasn't someone that wanted to be involved past a certain point...but I had no problem getting to that "point." My protective selfishness would only let me receive, never give. For so long, I'd tried to be "the nice guy," the *gentleman* that treated every woman like a lady, with a respect that never had to be earned, only given by the sheer fact that she had a certain biological make up; the guy my father is and my mother taught me to be. Apparently, that guy flourished forty years ago. But somewhere between Reaganomics, the crack epidemic, mass incarceration, reality television, twerk "music," and mumble rap, that guy was relegated to fictitious love novels and almost mythic 1950s television and film.

I admit it—I disheveled and disrupted the lives of a few in the wake of *Hurricane Me*. Those unsuspecting souls who had gotten caught up in the whirlwind romance that I had been only months prior. I witnessed the hopeful romantics' eyes, filled with expectation of the blossoming fruit that had finally ripened in season; only to find, once fruition manifested, the cankerworm and locust had already had their way with me. "Don't fall for me; you're dealing with damaged goods," I would admonish. In my mind, doing this relieved me of the burden of guilt. At that point, she makes a grownup decision to trespass my junkyard heart at her own risk. Deceptively, the allure and idea of something you shouldn't have is more rewarding than actually having it.

I actually thought what I was doing was okay as long as I cautioned early on that I had no interest in being anything more than "friends." **I would never want to do anyone the way I was done...I was blindsided,** was my thinking, so I would let them know. (But why get involved at all?? Why even take it *to* a certain point without having intentions of delivering expectations? As a man, are you not in control of yourself, your impulses, and your actions?) I'd become as skilled as any musician, able to pluck her heartstrings in an attempt to play only *my* favorite song, never minding the fact there were always a few sour notes from a heart out of tune. But inevitably, history repeats its lessons like questions wrongly answered until they are answered correctly. As I asked, so they asked: **What are we? What are we doing? Where are we going with this?** I recognized the despair in their eyes and the concern in their voices; it was my own only months prior. I'd almost copied my paramour's answer verbatim: the words ***wondering aimlessly*** came to mind to say, but I almost choked on the venomous words as they came up. Dear G-D...what have I done?? "Train up a child in the way he should go, even when he is old he will not depart from it." (Prov. 22:6) As a dog on a leash, I was jerked back to the teachings of my mother and the example of my father. **Who have I become?? I am not this person...I can't play games where matters of the heart are concerned.** I never realized...hurt people, hurt people; damaged people, damage people; broken people, break people. Whether the intent is there or not, the event occurs. I had to ask forgiveness for what I'd done...and with that, I had to forgive what was done to me...

Maybe it was your kindness,
maybe it was your smile;
maybe it was the fact that I'm lonely
and it's been a while.
Maybe I was just blinded or maybe
it was your eyes,
staring into mine, so deeply, you could
see my mind and what I'm thinking.
It's probably not exactly what you're hoping for;
I'm on the fence and the more time spent,
just leaves you wanting more.
Hopelessness won't set in, so you
keep holding on.
I notice this, so just like the wind,
I guess I'm moving on.
'Cuz I aint tryna play no games witcha;
I'm backing out the frame, hoping that
you get the picture.
Cupid's lacking aim—missed me, but I
guess he hit ya;
and I don't play with heartstrings, I am
no musician.
I'm a man, and as such, I understand
G-D's dream;

SITUATIONSHIPS

*so I ain't tryna take advantage of
another king's queen.
Matters not if you don't know him yet,
you don't belong to me.
Yeah, it's been great so far but just
because you're good
doesn't mean you're good for me...
(I'm sorry)*

-SaeLah

19
.god Is Second Best.
"...suffer the little children to come unto Me..."
-Rabbi Yeshua

Separations in and of themselves are hard...more so when children are involved. Children love with a love that comes from the purest of places. Intellect is no match for innocence—they can't comprehend why some grownups just don't work together.

Her daughter and I formed quite the bond. From secret handshakes and flying kites at the park, to picking her up after school, movies on "five dollar Tuesdays," gymnastics and cheer competitions, I wanted to be there for it all. I reveled in the chance to be the same type of father my father is. We were thick as thieves from genesis. But with the revelation of her mother and me, where does that leave us? Being so young and impressionable, how would the trajectory of her life go seeing another man and father figure leave? I had no answers to questions like, *Do I still try and work at a relationship with her since there is no longer a relationship with the mother??*

SITUATIONSHIPS

Does she know why I don't come around as much anymore? How will this all impact her view of the family dynamic, long term? (Maybe these are questions EVERY man who contemplates being a deadbeat dad should ask) Maybe I am too analytical. But I loved her as if she were my own…she was, even if but for a moment in time..

To the daughter I never had
but always wanted: just know that
you were wanted.
Just know I've often wondered what
life would be like if I'd entered your
life just two and a half years prior...
just prior to mommy meeting the man
of her dreams and unfortunately,
the nightmare of her reality.
If I'd been there, I could've protected
mommy from the pain of a broken
heart and shielded your eyes so you
never would've had to have seen mommy
cry.
You would've only seen what it looks like
for a real man to pursue a real woman,
and not see that same man made to wait
and pay for the previous man's mistakes.
You would've known a real man
ALWAYS
gives more so you should never settle
for less.
You would've known how a man treats
a woman;
how a king treats a queen; how a
gentleman treats a lady, and as such,
you are.
See, I looked forward to awkward

*daddy-daughter discussions and already
anticipated answers to questions like,
"How do I know he's the one?"
And that's when I smile, look you in
your eyes and reply,
"When you no longer have to ask that
question...just like me and mommy all those
years ago. So let us serve as your example.
And the only question that remains,
hanging in the air is the question that leaps
from his lips when he asks,
'Will you marry me?'"
See, I looked forward to forever with
mommy by my side and you in my arms,
armed with nothing but a "Superman complex"
and the will to protect.
NO "step"—just "Father."
No one needs to know the difference,
people say we look alike anyway.
"I can tell you get your height from him,"
they say.
(But if they only knew)
I guess our spirits are kindred,
and with all the time spent together in the
past year it's no wonder our spirits take on
similar characteristics.
Maybe that's why I think you're so perfect,
because your spirit looks exactly like mine.
(My beautiful baby girl)
One day (dooms day lol), you're going to grow
up and shed the cocoon of adolescence and
take on the wings of womanhood.
Stretch them far.
Flap them strong in the wind of*

SITUATIONSHIPS

*independence and as you soar to heights unimaginable, never forget what keeps you grounded. Never forget, the man looking for you will always seek to preserve your purity and protect your innocence. Never forget to always obey mommy... and try your very best to never forget me. And I guess...if I can't officially be your father then, being 'god' [father] is second best.
(I accept)*

-SaeLah

20
Regrettably Yours.
"...in the end I ain't tryna live with regrets..."
- Dee-1

I'd been in this state of confusion for so long; so turned around by the whirlwind, I had no idea which way was up, bearings adrift. I felt like I was fighting Mike Tyson, and was turned around by a punch so hard, that I started swinging at the ref. I needed a familiar voice. I began questioning what was wrong with *me* that this would happen. You know, asking the hard questions.

I turned to a female friend who I'd known for years. She is a successful, attractive, and endearing young professional…someone *any* man would love to have in his life. As analytical as I am, my mind wandered like a four year old in the store in search of the toy section. Why not? Why had she been in my life all these years, and we never tried to take it *there*? What if I missed a great opportunity with an exceptional woman? Should I even shoot my shot now, or is the game over for that? If I didn't shoot it, would I have any regrets?

Dear you,

Lately...
I've been letting my emotions run...
(marathons)
until they bleed through a ballpoint pen
onto paper, regretting
how I missed opportunities to date you
repressing
past memories, I could've made you mine,
for all time like eternity.
And though the thoughts crossed my mind
before, recently it occurred to me:
we could've been the greatest love song
ever sung.
And everyone would've known all our lyrics
and tried their best to remix us but as you
know, nothing's ever as good as the original
so, our love would've remained the most
classic of love ballads.
But I can't grasp it...
how could I let love pass and not reach out
and grab it?
I guess I was passive and looking back at it
there's no doubt in my mind that we
could've lasted.
I'm tryna look past it but how do I manage
when it seems that I'm stuck in the past
looking backwards?
And it's hard to imagine but somehow
this rabbit has led me on trails like my
name was 'Alice...'

*But it's not.
So why am I still backpacking through
this land full of wonder?
But there's nothing wonderful about
always wondering how good it could've
been...would've been.
SHOULD've been.
Maybe I should've been more assertive,
less nervous; more forward,
less backward in my thinking,
thinking I didn't measure up, wasn't
enough, or maybe you were too much;
either way, I was less than you deserved
but...who am I to make that call for you?
Your fingers weren't broken so you should
have been able to dial destiny for yourself
if you wanted to.
And knowing me, I would've answered on
the first ring.
Maybe the second if I was mid-sentence
having a conversation with G-D, telling
him about this girl I'd met back on earth
who makes my heart do a Cheshire grin
EVERY time I hear her inhale.
And that's when He'll laugh at me and say,
"Son, I do believe you are smitten!
But that's okay because as it is written,
'the greatest of these is LOVE."
And as opportunity knocks and destiny
calls, He looks at me and smiles saying,
"Speak of the 'angel' now...It's her."
And when I answer, your voice on the
other end says, "Well it took you long
enough!"*

SITUATIONSHIPS

And the rest of our lives together isn't long
enough so He created eternity.
Internally, I know this is how it was supposed
to go and I froze.
I apologize.
I guess instead of taking that chance I stayed
where it was familiar, in that house built on
the sand;
and the wind blew and the rain came and
that house was washed away and I...
well I was left homeless without a love
to call my own, it's embarrassing really...
I have to be silly to grab for this pity,
but I'm poverty stricken and if I had a
penny for every time I smiled when the
wind whispered your name and I longed
to tell you our secrets...
I'd be giving Bill Gates a loan.
But alas, with open space to roam I've
ventured back into the ventricles of your
heart, hoping to make it my home with no
baggage from "past voyages," only this letter.
How I wish I would've penned it better,
because I still don't think you fully
understand.
I can count on one hand all my regrets
in this life;
and if I'd told you back then, I'm guessing
this life would have ended up being a lot
different for both of us.
So I'm hoping thus: that your friendship is
the least I have of you;
because friendship in the hand is worth a
relationship in the bush.

So let's promise never to end it,
like this letter.
Forever your friend
(was hoping for more)...

Sincerely,
Me...

Regrettably,
Yours...

<3

-SaeLah

21
Conversations.
"...make yourself have the hard conversations..."

When falling, one instinctively puts out their arms and hands in an attempt to catch themselves or break their fall. We embrace that which is closest to us that will secure or safeguard our wellbeing in that moment. This is completely natural and rational. You *should* do this or at the very least, brace for impact. However, the heart is not always rational. The heart is not a brain so it does not think; it is emotional, so it *feels*. It usually feels in the moment, not for the future. So, in the words of Jim Rohn, "Our emotions have to be as educated as our intellect." Our emotions must mature. Love is what I call "logically irrational." It should make sense that it doesn't make sense…or it doesn't make sense how it makes sense. Either way, your heart AND your head have to be involved, both present in the moment. All heart, and you'll be looking foolish; all head, and you will never recognize love when it is present. You have to acknowledge what you are feeling, and strategically (and rationally) work out what you should do about what it is you are feeling. Force yourself to have the hard conversations..

While entertaining her presence,
your guessing is first AND second,
stressing;
wishing the suggestions your head gives
your heart were only rumors sparked by
the most unreliable source.
And then it happens--
her cell tattle tells and flashing across
the top is a name that came up in previous
conversations that went like:
"He's a non-factor.
I'm moving past the 'past' with the 'present'
G-D has gifted my 'future' in you,
so you don't have to worry.
Yeah, I fell in love with him but I eventually
hit the bottom and since, you have been
my rock; I'm not leaving you."
But that phone chime rings in a tone
too tumultuous for my 10 oz heart
to take, even though it feels like it
weighs a ton...
I guess I'm heavy hearted...
Barely departed and the rumors have
started and such says my head to my heart:

[Head]:
"She never loved us.
We were just the SECOND hand that passed
the MINUTES of her life, a life we thought
would be 'OURS' together.
And these DAYS we're too WEAK to
triumph the MONTHS that have
turned into YEARS...

SITUATIONSHIPS

*years we've wasted and waited to
have all of her.
Heart, the rumors are true.
That phone call cements the somber
suspicion I had and already knew.
So here's what we'll do:
Form a coup and break out of this
mental prison she's left us in,
because forming new memories are
the only way I can release the old ones
that keep us trapped here,
so what do you say?"*

*[Heart]:
"Well, I've never been one for prison breaks.
WORD is, it's best to serve your full
SENTENCE in order to **pin point**
exactly where she's at
(no "PAIR OF GRAPHS")
{PARAGRAPHS}
But I've heard from other hearts,
waiting can make for a beautiful story..."*

Scripted, *so beautifully* **written**...
If you meant it, then why is this **fiction**?
If you **penned** *it, why didn't you finish?*
*"Finished."
What a* **novel** *idea...
Who am I to break* **character**?
Although, this was no **fairy tale**...

"Situationships" rarely are...

-SaeLah

22
.Designer Clothes.
(Afterword)

*I wish I was a much better dresser.
Maybe then, I'd be able to clothe
my thoughts of You with designer
words worthy of Your affection.
As it stands, my thoughts are naked,
streaking across the fields of my mind
with no words to clothe or express them.
Earthly words inadequately express my
reflections, for example: how does one
accurately depict the sunsets of the heavens
placed carefully inside Your retinas??
I can't.
It seems I'm stuck with the simplest syntax.
Or maybe, when You enter my mind
words run and hide.
Your brilliance makes them scatter like*

roaches and too much light blinds!
Honestly, the only logical explanation
is that there are no words to define or
describe Your greatness, it can only be
experienced.
Don't worry, the secrets to what we have
are safe with me...they'll have to be—
I couldn't tell them if I had to, wanted to,
or even tried.
But every time I experience You, my eyes
try to articulate it when they whisper words
worth uttering because I cry.
Can You hear my tears scream of Your
goodness?
Can You hear them shout Your affection
towards me??
Can You hear them?
They worship in a whisper unworthy of
the words of this wretched man's mind.
My thoughts of You are clothed in the most
ragged of words compared to what I truly
feel for you...but they are all I have,
all I can offer.
You have authored my beginning and
penned my end.
There is none like You.
Sometimes, silently I sit in Your presence,
simply because I am at a loss for words.
Words...
the very things that are capable of building
worlds or breaking hearts.
Words...
able to hurt and heal with one utterance...
Words...

things that declare
war and peace,
love and hate,
joy and pain;
able to bless and curse,
give life and death...
Words...
Words.
There is an art and a certain sense of
fashion that is needed in order to
assemble letters into words,
words into sentences,
and sentences into paragraphs that
clothe the thoughts I have toward You.
So since nothing fits, peer through the
windows of my soul into the mind of my
heart as my thoughts lay bare before
Thee,
oh L-RD...

-SaeLah

___

Eventually, I stopped falling. I woke up cognizant, fully conscious and relatively healed. Upon impact, I was broken…however, I realized I did not die as I previously thought I would. "Bottom" was a lot softer than I'd anticipated. With eyes lifted, it occurred to me that I was in G-D's hands. He'd caught me and would not allow me to hit the bottom. I was clay, broken…but broken *in* the hands of the Potter, "so He was able to remake me into another vessel, as it pleased Him to make" (Jeremiah 18:2-4). I cannot remember the day that I stopped hurting. I only know one day, I realized it'd been weeks since I even fashioned a thought of *Her*. Somehow, I'd moved on…I was lucky. Some people can only move past it…but never move on.

For me, the solution was never as simple as finding a new one to get over an old one. That only leaves a trail of hurt and shattered hearts in your wake who will go and do likewise. Again, "hurt people will hurt people." The only way is to face your fears of rejection, loneliness, bitterness, unforgiveness, and brokenness head on. Acknowledge the very real fact that it happened. And then, close your eyes and take a deep breath and acknowledge the very real fact that it is no longer happening. *Acknowledge*, but do not dwell. I know it hurts. I once heard a minister Paula White say, "A wounding is an event, healing is a process. The deeper the wound [pain], the longer the process [healing]." It will take time. It will take endurance. It will take intentionality. But you do NOT have to remain broken. The Potter will fix you. You don't have to remain hurt. Allow the Great Physician to heal you. One of my favorite quotes regarding love comes from Thornton Wilder:

> *Without your wounds where would your power be?*
> *It is your melancholy that makes your low voice tremble into the hearts of men and women.*
> *The very angels themselves cannot persuade the wretched and blundering children on earth as can one human being broken on the wheels of living.*
> **In Love's service, only wounded soldiers can serve.** *Physician, draw back.*

Embrace your scars. Some see scars as a reminder of the hurt that happened to them. Others see scars as evidence that something has healed. It's all about perspective.

Another of my favorite quotes with regard to love comes from the brilliant C.S. Lewis. In his book, *The Four Loves*, he writes:

> *To love at all is to be vulnerable.*
> *Love anything, and your heart will be*
> *wrung and possibly broken.*
> *If you want to be sure of keeping*
> *your heart intact you must give your*
> *heart to no one, not even an animal.*
> *Wrap it carefully around with hobbies*
> *and little luxuries, avoid all entanglements.*
> *Lock it up safely in the casket of your selfishness.*
> *And in that casket, safe, dark, motionless, airless,*
> *it will become unbreakable, impenetrable and*
> *irredeemable.*
> **The only place outside of heaven where you**
> **can be perfectly safe from the dangers of love**
> **is Hell.**

Lewis brings up a very interesting and important point—the issue of vulnerability. To love is to be vulnerable. Don't permit past let downs to cause your heart to be callous. Love harder. Don't draw back. Don't give another person so much power over you that it causes you to change the way you love and love without vulnerability. This is not protection or self-preservation, this is selfishness and in the harvest of love, even the smallest weed of selfishness will destroy your crop.

Is it possible to avoid *situationships*? Perhaps, but the threat is always looming at the beginning of any relationship. But don't let the threat make you put up walls. The same wall that keeps out disappointment could be keeping out happiness. I suppose there are signs to watch for but I think major points to be intentional about are clearly defined answers to the "what are we" question and establishing boundaries. I know these days it is very popular not to subscribe to any particular label, but labels do have a place. Your name is a label. If something has your name on it, I doubt very much you would want someone else tampering with it. The same is true of the heart. If there are benefits to having your heart belong to a soulmate, why let a situationship experience those benefits? It doesn't take too long to know whether or not you could see yourself with someone long term (but it does take time). So, being able to answer the "what are we" and "what are we doing" questions will give perspective and also let you know which label to assign to that person, so you can then know which benefits to give! "Friends with benefits" situations(hips) are stupid. If I am married, why would my homie or friend get the EXACT same benefits package as my *wife*? Even though you may not have met "the one" yet, there should be certain things that are saved for "the one," in preparation for the "the one." Move away from #Situationships so you can live in #REALationships (the next book, coming soon lol).

I pray you have been encouraged. I pray you do not lose hope nor waver in faith. I pray you move past the scars of situationships previously encountered, and I pray you love with the same intensity as when you first loved. I pray you be diligent where matters of the heart are concerned, not naïve; and I pray The Creator continues to write your story...He loves to write romance novels and they are *always* best sellers.

;-)

-SaeLah

SaeLah

ABOUT THE AUTHOR

SaeLah is a Louisiana native. At age 11, he started writing poetry and even started writing his own songs, and since has written thousands of verses. An affinity for the arts, mainly music, poetry, and acting, was developed in him at an early age and landed him on season five of TV One's program, *Verses and Flow*. "I just want to use my gift of words to glorify my Creator and edify His people," he says.

Poet, author, songwriter, rapper, musician, motivational speaker, gentleman, scholar, lover, fighter, and now actor, SaeLah is one to look for in the coming times as he promises, this is only the beginning. He currently resides in Atlanta, Ga.

For more on SaeLah, please visit www.saelahunplugged.com.

Made in the USA
Columbia, SC
09 March 2018